TOOLS FOR TEACHERS

- **ATOS:** 0.8
- **GRL:** C
- **WORD COUNT:** 29
- **CURRICULUM CONNECTIONS:** animals, habitats

Skills to Teach

- **HIGH-FREQUENCY WORDS:** a, are, call, in, them, these, they, we, what
- **CONTENT WORDS:** babies, baby, climb, cuddle, find, food, forest, kits, live, play, squirrels, tree
- **PUNCTUATION:** periods, question mark
- **WORD STUDY:** long /a/, spelled *ay* (*play*); long /e/, spelled ee (*tree*); /oo/, spelled oo (*food*); multisyllable words (*babies*, *cuddle*, *forest*, *squirrels*)
- **TEXT TYPE:** information report

Before Reading Activities

- Read the title and give a simple statement of the main idea.
- Have students "walk" though the book and talk about what they see in the pictures.
- Introduce new vocabulary by having students predict the first letter and locate the word in the text.
- Discuss any unfamiliar concepts that are in the text.

After Reading Activities

The book tells us that baby squirrels are called kits. Did the children know this before reading the book? Can they name any other baby animals that have different names than their parents? Sound out each new word. Write their answers on the board.

Tadpole Books are published by Jump!, 5357 Penn Avenue South, Minneapolis, MN 55419, www.jumplibrary.com

Editor: Jenna Trnka **Designer:** Anna Peterson

Photo Credits: Rosa Jay/Shutterstock, cover; Robert Eastman/Shutterstock, 1; Gay Bumgarner/Alamy, 2–3, 16tm; GlobalP/iStock, 4–5; Jef Wodniack/iStock, 6–7, 16bl; Catalin Petolea/Shutterstock, 8–9, 16br; Pi-Lens/Shutterstock, 10–11 (foreground), 16tl; Dmitrii Brodovoi/Shutterstock, 10–11 (background), 16tr; Design Pics Inc/Alamy, 12–13, 16bm; Sue Feldberg/Dreamstime, 14–15.

Library of Congress Cataloging-in-Publication Data
Names: Nilsen, Genevieve, author.
Title: Squirrel kits / by Genevieve Nilsen.
Description: (Tadpole edition). | Minneapolis, MN : Jump!, Inc., (2018) | Series: Forest babies | Includes index.
Identifiers: LCCN 2018007773 (print) | LCCN 2017061707 (ebook) | ISBN 9781624969782 (ebook) | ISBN 9781624969768 (hardcover : alk. paper) | ISBN 9781624969775 (pbk.)
Subjects: LCSH: Squirrels—Infancy—Juvenile literature.
Classification: LCC QL737.R68 (print) | LCC QL737.R68 N55 2018 (ebook) | DDC 599.3613/92—dc23
LC record available at https://lccn.loc.gov/2018007773

FOREST BABIES

SQUIRREL KITS

by Genevieve Nilsen

TABLE OF CONTENTS

tadpole books

SQUIRREL KITS

These babies cuddle.

What are they?

Baby squirrels.

We call them kits.

tree

They live in a tree.

They climb.

They play.

They find food in the forest.

WORDS TO KNOW

climb

cuddle

forest

kits

play

tree

INDEX